ST PETERSBURG
THE CITY AT A GLANCE

Troitskiy Bridge
Ornate and elegant, the metalwork above is
a riot of civic symbolism. Constructed in 1903
(the 200th anniversary of the city's founding),
it spans the Neva in five giant metal arches.

Summer Gardens
Wooded walks thronged by statues host
Peter the Great's Summer Palace, a modest
structure designed by Domenico Trezzini.

Marsovo Pole
The 'Field of Mars' was once a parade ground
filled with imperial guards stomping up and
down to the nearby barracks. It's now home
to the Eternal Flame of the Revolution.

Engineer's Castle
Also known as the Mikhailovsky Castle,
this home to the overspill from the Russian
Museum (see p033) was first built to protect
assassination-phobic Paul I: it didn't work.

Marble Palace
Housing yet another offshoot of the Russian
Museum (including many modern paintings),
the palace gets its name from the 32 types of
marble that clad its Antonio Rinaldi façades.

Russian Museum
Sprawling, varied and stuffed with treasures,
the museum was kick-started with a selection
of works from the Hermitage (see p010), plus
many more purloined after the revolution.
See p033

Church on Spilled Blood
Tributes don't come much more OTT than this
Orthodox church, started in 1883 and sweated
over for 25 years, a monument to the spot
where Alexander II was killed by a grenade.
See p012

INTRODUCTION
THE CHANGING FACE OF THE URBAN SCENE

St Petersburg's horizon of golden spires eventually gives way to a vista of steam-belching chimneys, giant cranes and looming workers' housing, a reminder of its past as the Soviet industrial powerhouse. The capital enjoys a three-century-old reputation for combining culture and cavorting, intertwined with some of the most fraught military and political histories of any city on earth. Founded in 1703 as a strategic bulwark against the advancing Swedes, St Petersburg grew from fortress into metropolis, thanks to Peter the Great's penchant for Western idealism.

Despite Stalin's brutality and a generation-defining siege in WWII, the city's core still bears the hallmarks of Swiss architect Domenico Trezzini and Italians Carlo Rossi and Bartolomeo Rastrelli, who gave it an extraordinary combination of classical and baroque over the course of a century. It helps that it's home to the Hermitage (see p010), one of the world's foremost treasure houses, and an unparalleled collection of classical architecture, baroque palaces and neo-Russian churches. Add to the mix a thriving bar and nightclub scene, internationally rated hotels and a population ever eager to embrace the midsummer 'white nights', when darkness becomes an eternal dusk, and you have a destination that's poised to pique curiosity and reward hedonism. There's a real feeling that this city is finally ready to put the dismal 20th century behind it and enter the next stage of its life.

ESSENTIAL INFO

FACTS, FIGURES AND USEFUL ADDRESSES

TOURIST OFFICE
City Tourist Information Centre
12 Dvortsovaya Ploshchad
T 310 2231
www.ctic.spb.ru

TRANSPORT
Car hire
Avis
T 327 5418
Hertz
T 326 4505
Metro
urbanrail.net/eu/pet/petersbg
Taxis
Taxi Blues
T 271 8888
Neva Taxi
T 053

EMERGENCY SERVICES
Ambulance
T 03
Fire
T 01
Police
T 02
24-hour pharmacy
American Medical Clinic
78 Naberezhnaya Reki Moyki
T 740 2090
www.amclinic.ru

CONSULATES
British Consulate-General
5 Proletarskoy Diktatury Ploshchad
T 320 3200
www.britishembassy.gov.uk
US Consulate-General
15 Furshtatskaya Ulitsa
T 331 2600
stpetersburg.usconsulate.gov

MONEY
American Express
23 Malaya Morskaia Ulitsa
T 326 4500
travel.americanexpress.com

POSTAL SERVICES
Post Office
9 Pochtamskaya Ulitsa
T 312 7460 or 312 8302
Shipping
UPS
T 703 3939
www.ups.com

BOOKS
The Bronze Horseman by Alexander
Pushkin (Bristol Classical Press)
Petersburg Perspectives by Frank
Althaus, Mark Sutcliffe and Yury
Molodkovets (Booth-Clibborn Editions)
Crime and Punishment by Fyodor
Dostoyevsky (Penguin Books)
St Petersburg by Colin Amery and Brian
Curran (Frances Lincoln)

WEBSITES
Newspapers
www.kommersant.com
www.sptimes.ru

COST OF LIVING
Taxi from Pulkovo Airport to city centre
€35
Cappuccino
€2.40
Packet of cigarettes
€0.90
Daily newspaper
€0.35
Bottle of champagne
€350

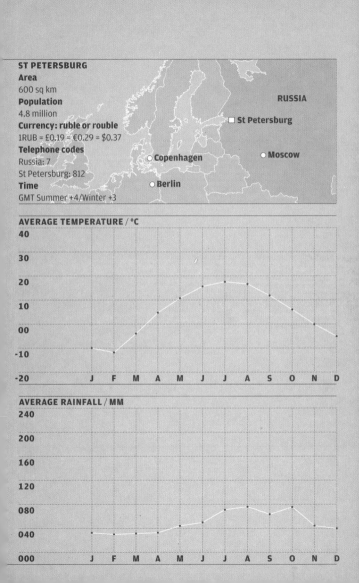

ST PETERSBURG
Area
600 sq km
Population
4.8 million
Currency: ruble or rouble
1RUB = £0.19 = €0.29 = $0.37
Telephone codes
Russia: 7
St Petersburg: 812
Time
GMT Summer +4/Winter +3

RUSSIA

☐ St Petersburg

○ Moscow

○ Copenhagen

○ Berlin

AVERAGE TEMPERATURE / °C

40												
30												
20												
10												
00												
-10												
-20	J	F	M	A	M	J	J	A	S	O	N	D

AVERAGE RAINFALL / MM

240												
200												
160												
120												
080												
040												
000	J	F	M	A	M	J	J	A	S	O	N	D

NEIGHBOURHOODS

THE AREAS YOU NEED TO KNOW AND WHY

To help you navigate the city, we've chosen the most interesting districts (see the map inside the back cover) and underlined featured venues in colour, according to their location (see below); those venues that are outside these areas are not coloured.

VASILYEVSKIY ISLAND

Designated as the heart of the city by Peter the Great before the action moved south, this is the largest island created by the Neva river. Peter's vision included canals and bridges – he was an admirer of Venice and Amsterdam. Many of the city's oldest buildings are here, such as the Central Naval Museum (4 Birzhevaya Ploshchad, T 328 2502) and the early 1800s Rostral Columns that flank it, used to guide ships.

PETROGRADSKAYA STORONA

This district is shaped by the impressive ramparts of the Peter and Paul Fortress (Petropavlovskaya Krepost), the first building in the newly founded city, at the lower end of this spit of land. At its heart is Aleksandrovskiy Park, which boasts the Botanical Gardens (2 Professora Popova Ulitsa, T 234 1764), while the embankment to the east is full of fashionable places to eat and club, with shopping to the north.

SENNAYA PLOSHCHAD

Due south of St Isaac's Square, this area was St Petersburg's original hay market, a spirited district that was equal parts free enterprise and grinding poverty. Today, upmarket boutiques are springing up along Voznesenskiy Prospekt. To the south is Naberezhnaya Reki Fontanki, one of the finest stretches of waterside property in the city. The Fontanka canal runs in a loop from east to west, forming a boundary between the historic core and the suburbs.

PALACE EMBANKMENT

It's a pleasant walk via the back streets between the Hermitage (see p010) and the Marsovo Pole – the 'Field of Mars' that was the imperial parade ground. Nearby are the Summer Gardens, housing Peter's Summer Palace (T 314 0456), and the onion domes of the Church on Spilled Blood (see p012).

GOSTINYY DVOR

The city's main shopping street, Nevskiy Prospekt, runs through this district. It's part ceremonial route, part awe-inspiring architecture and, in places, drenched in tat. The city is a massively improved retail destination, but Nevskiy isn't the cutting edge. It's a useful navigation tool, though.

NEW HOLLAND

This central triangular site is bounded by canals and was formerly a vast complex of 18th-century, navy-owned warehouses. Redevelopment promises a modern art museum, apartments and more, all under the watchful eye of Lord Foster, no less, whose ambitious scheme for a brand-new cultural centre should be open by 2009.

ADMIRALTY

Bang in the centre of the city, it is here that the architecture is at its most imposing. The navy's former HQ in Adrian Zakharov's Admiralty building (1 Admiralteyskiy Prospekt) was designed as a feast of spires and columns; and here you stand at the intersection of the city's main routes.

LANDMARKS

THE SHAPE OF THE CITY SKYLINE

St Petersburg is not short of landmarks, although the ardent modernist would do well to note that architectural innovation stopped dead about two centuries ago. That isn't to say there aren't contemporary gems to be found, but the focus is rightfully on the palaces, cathedrals, churches and, most importantly, museums that gave this great city its international reputation. Often dubbed the 'Venice of the North', the city was built at great human cost. The workers who formed St Petersburg's foundations literally carved it out of the marshes, driving in wooden piles and building up the land to provide a stable base. Thousands died in the process, in atrocious conditions, even if today they remain only as an eerie, distant memory in a city that feels hewn from carved stone.

From the Peter and Paul Fortress (Petropavlovskaya Krepost, open 10am-6pm, Thursday-Tuesday), Peter the Great's new city radiated out, with the broad Fontanka, Griboedov and Moyka canals on the other side of the river providing a convenient series of zones into which architects, who were imported from Italy and Switzerland by Peter the Great, poured in their rigorous façades, squares and piazzas. From a distance, the exteriors are enticing, but up close, the ravages of years of harsh climate are laid bare. It's also a city of extremes – the canals jam with ice in the bitter winters and the sun barely scrapes the horizon in the summer. *For full addresses, see Resources.*

The Hermitage

Superlatives run out when it comes to this monument to the collectomania of Catherine the Great, which began in 1764. The museum (closed Mondays) is now an overflowing, self-contained fiefdom. Expansion is in the works, with Rem Koolhaas' OMA consulting on a radical reorganisation with local firm Studio 44. *2 Dvortsovaya Ploshchad, T 710 9079, www.hermitagemuseum.org*

Church on Spilled Blood

Perhaps St Petersburg's most distinctive landmark, this variously named church (sometimes it's called the Cathedral of the Resurrection of Christ) is an exuberant confection of polychrome cladding and onion domes. Built by Alexander III in memory of his father, whose blood really was spilled here, the neo-Russian style is far removed from the austere classicism of its surroundings, especially the façade clad in religious panels. It's the interior that really stuns, with every square inch coated in rich coloured mosaics, depicting biblical scenes. No wonder the Soviets promptly shut the structure in the 1930s and left it to rot. In the 1970s, it became a museum of mosaics, before reverting to the city's foremost tourist attraction.
2 Naberezhnaya Kanala Griboedova, T 315 1636, www.cathedral.ru

Finland Station

Peter the Great was mad about railways and he chose the British model as the one most suited to his new city. Dotted around you have Warsaw Station, Moscow Station, Ladozhsky Station and, up in the northeast, Finland Station (above). Few of St Petersburg's structures embody the stripped-down classicism of high Stalinist style as perfectly as this monument to the socialist glories of rail travel. The original building was the scene of Lenin's triumphant return to the city in April 1917, and the lucky train is now preserved, Hirst-like, in its own glass case. The new structure went up in the 1950s and the style has worn rather well – the austere façade, central clock tower and elaborate murals of lines and destinations (overleaf) all have a certain period charm.
6 Lenina Ploshchad

СХЕМА ДВИЖЕНИЯ ПОЕЗДОВ ДАЛЬНЕ

ГРОДНО
ВИЛЬНЮС РИГА ПСКОВ ТАЛЛИНН НАРВА ИВАН-ГОРОД
КАЛИНИНГРАД ДАУГАВПИЛС ПЫТАЛОВО ПЛЮССА
ПОЛОЦК СЕБЕЖ ЛУГА
ВИТЕБСК НОВОСОКОЛЬНИКИ ОРЕДЕЖ ДНО
НОВГОРОД УГЛОВКА
БАРАНОВИЧИ НЕВЕЛЬ СОБЛАГО
ОРША БОЛОГОЕ
КАТОВИЦЕ БРЕСТ МИНСК ВЕЛ.ЛУКИ РЖЕВ
ЛЬВОВ СОЛИГОРСК БРЯНСК
МОГИЛЕВ СМОЛЕНСК ОРЕЛ
ХАРЬКОВ КУРСК
ЧЕРНОВЦЫ БЕЛГОРОД
СИМФЕРОПОЛЬ ДЖАНКОЙ ПАВЕЛЕЦ
ДОНЕЦК
ЖЛОБИН ЕВПАТОРИЯ ЕЙСК РОСТОВ
ОВРУЧ СЕВАСТОПОЛЬ МАРИУПОЛЬ
ФЕОДОСИЯ СТАРОМИНСКАЯ ВОРОНЕЖ
КРАСНОДАР
КИЕВ АРМАВИР
ГОМЕЛЬ ТУАПСЕ

СЛЕДОВАНИЯ С ВО

МУРМА

ЕЛЬСИНКИ

АПАТИТЫ

ПЕТРОЗАВОДСК

КО

БЕЛОМОРСК

ВОЛОГДА

ВОЖЕГА

ОВСТРОЙ

ЛОДЕЙНОЕ ПОЛЕ

КОТЕЛЬНИЧ

КОШТА

ЧЕРЕПОВЕЦ

ЧЕПЦА

П

БАБАЕВО

КТ-ПЕТЕРБУРГ

КОСТРОМА

ГОРЬКИЙ

КИРОВ

РОВИЧИ

ИВАНОВО

ИЖЕВСК

НИ

ЧКОВО

ЯРОСЛАВЛЬ

КОВРОВ

ШУМЕРЛЯ

ЯЛЬ

АРЗАМАС

ВЛАДИМИР

СЕРГАЧ

МУРОМ

НАВАШИНО

РУЗАЕВКА

ОСКВА

ЯЗАНЬ

САРАНСК

ЯЖСК

ТАМБОВ

АСТРАХА

САРАТОВ

УРБАХ

HOTELS

WHERE TO STAY AND WHICH ROOMS TO BOOK

Accommodation is not a problem in St Petersburg, although for decades the balance tipped towards the grand end of the scale, unless you *really* wanted to slum it in an Intourist-approved hotel (www.intouristhotel.com). All that changed, naturally, when the big chains moved in and plastered cheap rooms all over the town. Today, small independent hoteliers are a more adventurous way of getting an intimate introduction to the city. However, a quality room is going to cost – disproportionately so when compared to some of the city's other prices – so it's worth staking out the better establishments and doing the trip in style. Happily, the compact centre means it's fairly easy to stay close to the action, and the best hotels are within walking distance of the main sights.

The city's top establishment, the Grand Hotel Europe (opposite), lends a much-needed air of respectability to Nevskiy Prospekt, its grandeur belying its role in the city's 1970s counterculture, when students and artists thronged the ground-floor café. Elsewhere, this fusion of arty style and elegance has long gone, as today more progressive design is the hallmark of independent cafés and clubs, leaving marble foyers to fashion shows and society parties.

However, new ventures are sprouting up all the time, adding to the city's many pensions and apartments, to create a breed of small-scale hotel perfectly pitched at boutique-minded travellers. *For full addresses and room rates, see Resources.*

Grand Hotel Europe

Occupying a corner site on the edge of Iskusstv Ploshchad, the Grand Hotel Europe has an impressive atrium and copious bars and restaurants. The main structure was created by combining several of Carlo Rossi's existing mansions and hotels with the Hotel de L'Europe in the middle of the 19th century, and opened properly in 1875. The turn of the 20th century saw further renovations by Fyodor Lidval, who also designed the Hotel Astoria (see p018). Now operating as part of the Orient Express Group, who renamed it in 1991, the vast suites, such as the Lidval (above) contain authentic antiques and paintings. A place to meet as well as stay, the hotel is a throwback to old Europe, and none the worse for that.
1/7 Mikhaylovskaya Ulitsa, T 329 6000, www.grandhoteleurope.com

Hotel Astoria

Situated opposite St Isaac's Cathedral, the Astoria combines old-world elegance with excellent restaurants and facilities, and has acquired a reputation as a spot to host big-name fashion launches and parties. The Astoria's 223 rooms are split into categories and colours, such as the red Superior Deluxe (right), and include 24 suites, while the best rooms are 715 to 724, high on the 7th floor. Then there are five Presidential Suites, named after composers (Tchaikovsky, Rachmaninov, Prokofiev, Shostakovich and Stravinsky), copious banqueting suites, conference rooms and ballrooms, a spa and 24-hour gym and the Davidov restaurant. Jazz and blinis make cold spring afternoons fly by. An enduring rumour claims Hitler planned to celebrate Leningrad's fall in this hotel, an ambition the city thwarted at great cost.
39 Bolshaya Morskaya Ulitsa, T 494 5757, www.astoria.spb.ru

Eliseev Palace Hotel

Pitched at the visitor hoping to sample a slice of St Petersburg's Tsarist opulence, the 2003 Eliseev Palace Hotel occupies a former merchant's palace that had served time as the city's House of Arts after the revolution. Today, the most revolutionary elements are the stratospheric prices, which reflect the quality of the restoration, the sheer scale of the rooms, of which the best are the two Eliseev Suites (bedroom, above), and the facilities (including a gym, Russian *banya*, Finnish sauna, casino and cigar lounge). The 6th-floor Victoria Restaurant offers Russian cuisine. The owners also run the new Residence Taleon Sheremetev Palace (T 324 9911), once the home of Count Alexander Sheremetev and now Russia's first private palace for rent. *59 Naberezhnaya Reki Moyki, T 324 9911, www.eliseevpalacehotel.com*

Corinthia Nevskij Palace Hotel

Given its location, the Corinthia doesn't have to try too hard, and if you're not in the mood for sub-John Portman-style amateur dramatics, this might not be your kind of hotel. But there's a lot to be said for the lobby (above), all giant chandeliers and ultra-efficient concierges. The hotel was one of the first out of the blocks after the fall of communism in 1991. Overhauled in 1993, the new structure combined a mansion and two existing hotels with a slab of chunky glass modernism that reeks of rampant capitalism. The hotel contains its own shopping mall and the Samoilov Family Museum, dedicated to the acting dynasty who lived on the site. There are five places to dine, including the award-winning Landskrona Restaurant. *57 Nevskiy Prospekt, T 380 2001, www.corinthia.ru*

Renaissance St Petersburg Baltic Hotel

Opened in 2004 under the Marriott banner, this hotel has managed to retain a boutique-like feel. The impressive lobby opens up into a full-height glazed atrium in the centre of the hotel, while the 102 rooms are modestly furnished without the excess gilding many local operators call upon to conjure up class. Best of all is the location, just west of St Isaac's Square and minutes away from the Mariinsky Theatre (see p038) and the Hermitage (see p010). The best rooms are the bi-level suites, while if you'd like a romantic view, then just head up to the 6th-floor terrace (above) and bar, with its near unbeatable panorama of St Isaac's Cathedral. There's also the highly rated Canvas Restaurant, a fitness centre and two saunas.

4 Pochtamtskaya Ulitsa, T 380 4000, www.marriott.com

Kempinski Hotel Moika 22

Renovating former palaces is the upscale hotelier's bread and butter, and for many international chains, St Petersburg's lamentably run-down collection of real estate has provided serious bargains. The Moika 22, the latest Russian venture by the German hotel group, has turned a near-derelict neo-classical riverside palace, built in 1853 by Basil von Witte, into a 197-room hotel, with a rooftop restaurant on the 9th floor, the Bellevue Brasserie, and a Relaxation Centre on the terrace. The façade is all that's left of the original building, but the new hotel has embraced old-school Russian style, as you'll find out if you check in to the River View Executive Suite (above), or choose to partake of traditional afternoon tea. *22 Naberezhnaya Reki Moyki, T 335 9111, www.kempinski-st-petersburg.com*

Rachmaninov Antique Hotel

Describing itself as a 19th-century salon, this 19-room hotel is aimed squarely at those hankering after pre-revolutionary style. Decked out with antique furniture, especially in the lobby, meeting areas and breakfast room (above), the bedrooms are compact and relatively sparsely furnished. However, they're perfectly serviceable; the Belle Chambre rooms are the ones to go for, given their spectacular views over the Kazan Cathedral and the Griboedov canal. Our pick is the lovely Rachmaninov Lux (right), which has two adjoined rooms and a private balcony. Downstairs there is a gallery with rotating exhibitions from St Petersburg's modern artists. A cute café-bar completes the picture. Equidistant from The Hermitage (see p010) and the Russian Museum (see p033), this friendly hotel is an art lover's paradise.
5 Kazanskaya Ulitsa, T 571 7618, www.kazansky5.com

Angleterre Hotel

Although it's essentially a rather grand annexe to the Hotel Astoria (see p018), the Angleterre can certainly hold its own. A late 1990s plan to redevelop the entire site was thankfully nixed, so the structure retains its original charm. The Senator Suite, Deluxe Room and Junior Suite have the best views, while the downstairs Borsalino Brasserie (above) serves fine food with unhurried service (while you wait, marvel at the décor, designed, like the rest of the hotel, by Olga Polizzi). The club and casino next door complement the facilities at the Astoria and the 193 rooms are very comfortable. The hotel shares the Astoria's sense of old-world glamour, all hushed lounges, clacking high heels and endless people-watching.

24 Bolshaya Morskaya Ulitsa, T 494 5666, www.angleterrehotel.com

Alexander House

A boutique hotel in the true sense of the term, Alexander House is slightly off the beaten track along the Kryukov canal, not far from the Fontanka. Small, charming and discreet, it has 16 rooms, each named after a different city, such as Barcelona (overleaf), and decorated accordingly and not without humour. Reception rooms include a library, restaurant, central hall (above) and Japanese spa. Run by Alexander Zhukov and his family, the hotel is contained within an old mansion house, which was converted into an apartment building after the revolution. The clever renovation retains the mansion's scale but also has a homely feel, helped by the warm lounge and library. Guests keep returning, perhaps to stay in each one of the rooms.
27 Naberezhnaya Kryukova Kanala,
T 575 3877, www.a-house.ru

Barcelona Room, Alexander House

Art Hotel

This compact gem east of the Summer Gardens is better suited to those on a budget who are not too concerned with hanging out in a spacious lobby. Pleasingly archaic in its approach – for a start you have to really search for the front door, as it's hidden in a courtyard behind elaborate iron gates (left) – the Art Hotel takes its cue from the kind of guesthouse that once catered to the city's artistic classes. Currently the hotel has just 14 rooms, all draped in velvety fabrics and heavy furniture, including a Junior Suite (above) and main Suite, which comes with a piano. Big plans are afoot for expansion and the creation of new fitness facilities to bring the hotel up to the level of its peers. One to watch, if you can find it.
27/29 Mokhovaya Ulitsa, T 740 7585, www.art-hotel.ru

24 HOURS

SEE THE BEST OF THE CITY IN JUST ONE DAY

The beauty of St Petersburg is its relative compactness. Unless you're hellbent on visiting the grim-but-epic hulks of Brezhnev-era housing projects, the rusting remains of long-abandoned Soviet factories or even the collapsed and unfinished highway bridge to the north of the city, you can confine your sightseeing, shopping and refuelling to a fairly small section of districts. However, when you consider that the Hermitage (see p010) itself takes many days to give up all its treasures to the most obsessive art lover (and there are tour packages dedicated solely to this one museum), it's vital to pick and choose your targets well before embarking on a journey round the centre of the city.

St Petersburg is a city of bridges, and criss-crossing the various rivers and canals, whether on foot, by car or by boat, is an essential part of the experience. Be warned, however, that during the *belye noche* (white nights), which officially run from June 11 to July 2, all the major bridges on the Neva are raised for three hours from 2am, leaving you inevitably stranded on the wrong side. On the other hand, these summer months are a time of involuntary sleep deprivation, giving you the perfect opportunity to bar hop with alacrity. Combining culture and entertainment is almost expected in a city with an historically fast and loose attitude to alcohol, so be sure to pace yourself carefully to last the full day.

For full addresses, see Resources.

10.00 Russian Museum

A welcome counterpoint to the, at times, overwhelming Hermitage, this is the place to go if you would like a dose of constructivism from the likes of Kasimir Malevich, Vladimir Tatlin and Wassily Kandinsky. As the main repository for all forms of Russian art (there are over 6,000 icons), there's also a fine collection of paintings from the socialist realism school, the heroic works that celebrated the glories of working for the revolution. The building itself is one of Carlo Rossi's most Italianate designs. Originally the home of Grand Duke Mikhail Pavlovich, it became the national museum under the decree of Nicholas II in 1898. Collections of folk art, medals, sculpture, prints and drawings supplement the epic canvases. *4 Inzhenernaya Ulitsa, T 595 4248, www.rusmuseum.ru/eng*

12.30 Beluga Silver & Amber Boutique

Architect Anton Gorlanov's souvenir shop is typically over the top – you step into a faux birch glade, with log-clad walls and shelves groaning with fur hats and dripping with amber and the ubiquitous Fabergé-style eggs. If you have to buy examples of the local crafts, you might as well do it in style. Gorlanov is the court architect of St Petersburg's commercial renaissance, also responsible for the Morkovka restaurant (T 233 9635), the Onegin club/restaurant (see p055) and the Day&Night boutique (T 234 2300). Epitomising his visual approach, Day&Night draws its inspiration from the Microsoft Windows 'pipes' screensaver to create a dizzying space – pieces by Paul Smith and Dries van Noten hang in a venue shaped by countless mirrors and optical tricks.
5 Iskusstv Ploshchad, T 325 8264

13.30 St Isaac's Cathedral

A brisk trot up the 262 steps leading to the colonnades of St Isaac's Cathedral is a fine way to orient oneself in the city. The cathedral itself is a rather forbidding neo-classical lump of marble and granite, completed in 1858 and standing head and shoulders above the rest of the city. Its silhouette is visible from great distances across the Gulf of Finland. The piped music, swinging wildly between Shostakovich and marching bands, isn't to everyone's taste, but the view across the Neva to the great shipyard cranes, or back over the spires of the city, will keep you sane.
Isaakievskaya Ploshchad 1, T 315 9732

14.30 Krokodil

Kicking back in a Dostoyevsky-themed restaurant is one of the pleasures of St Petersburg's culture, which mixes high and low without a thought. Krokodil is jungle-themed, low ceilinged and pleasantly gloomy – dim lights and comfy chairs make it the perfect place for some beer-fuelled intellectualising over an unhurried Italian-style lunch.
18 Galernaya Ulitsa, T 314 9437

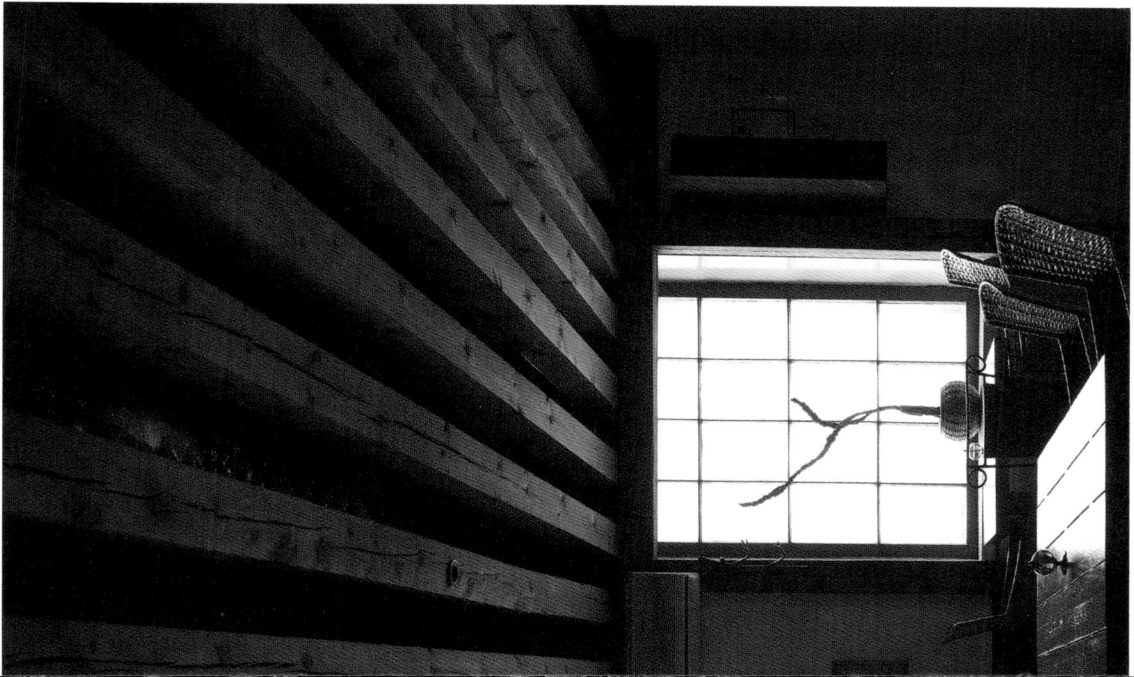

18.30 Mariinsky Theatre

With its origins in Catherine the Great's Imperial Opera and Ballet theatre, which opened in 1783, the current Mariinsky, housed in a building by Albert Cavos, dates from 1860. Once the world's largest auditorium, it has played host to the world's best ballet and opera, enjoying a second wind during the Soviet era when the art forms were democratised. Today the company is known worldwide as the Kirov and the theatre is still hugely respected. Spruce yourself up and be prepared to pay full whack – only locals get cheap tickets (the socialist artistic tradition doesn't seem to have died out). However, the Mariinsky is embarking on a massive and much-needed overhaul, so check it's open before planning your night.
1 Teatralnaya Ploshchad, T 326 4141, www.mariinsky.spb.ru

23.15 Decadence

If you're the type who thinks that 18,000 roubles (€530) is a fair price for a bottle of Cristal, then Decadence is the place for you. The no-nonsense name tells you all you need to know; this is monied hedonism of the kind that would make Marx spin in his grave. That said, Decadence is the best of the lot in St Petersburg's superclub league, a glamorous head and shoulders above the shabby (but friendly) art bars.

It should also be noted that one country's definition of class and elegance can often fall slightly short of another's. No matter, tuck into the international menu that runs until 6am (try the fish shashlik), before dancing and people-watching until dawn. *17a Sherbakov Pereulok, T 947 7070, www.decadence.spb.ru*

URBAN LIFE

CAFÉS, RESTAURANTS, BARS AND NIGHTCLUBS

The city's nightlife is legendary, with the white nights in summer providing almost perpetual light thanks to St Petersburg's status as one of the most northerly metropolises in the world. Naturally, this brings an upsurge of city dwellers onto the streets, as well as an influx of tourists eager for both the meteorological experience and the enhanced hospitality. The bar and nightclub scene moves fast, and the in-crowd's favourite place changes with predictable regularity. Smaller, more intimate venues are perhaps the most atmospheric, although new Russian money has resulted in a spate of elaborate superclubs, with some still going so far as to apply a policy of 'face control', the logical if rather totalitarian extension of dress code: if you don't look the part, you're not coming in.

The more adventurous traveller should keep their ear to the ground for news of out-of-town raves, not strictly legal but hugely popular with locals over the summer months. Usually held deep in the forest, or in old Cold War bunkers or warehouses, this is the one time the St Petersburg promoters set aside their differences and work together for a common goal. A famous party takes place at the ancient Fort Alexander, or Chumnoy, 30km and a boat ride out of town. For the rest of the year, clubs are sharply divided between the ultra-sleek venues packed with wall-to-wall designer threads and the grungier places that have sprung up in retaliation. *For full addresses, see Resources.*

Aquarel

This floating restaurant, which sits at the mouth of the Malaya Neva, was one of the city's first fusion venues. Highly successful under executive chef Christopher Presutti (who has since moved on), it is still very well rated in the gastronomic stakes. The menu features a generous smattering of fresh seafood and the static steel and glass boat offers diners an excellent view of the riverside architecture – and the heavy evening traffic heading out along Vasilyevskiy Island. On the top floor is Aquarelissimo, a more affordable bistro serving Mediterranean food. The location also makes it a top coffee spot, if you don't feel like dipping into the pricey menus. Regular DJ nights and the occasional concert fill out the restaurant's schedule. *14a Dobrolubova Prospekt, T 320 8600, www.aquarel.net*

Platforma Art Café
Providing a fusion of all that the city's artier citizens love best, this café, bar, restaurant, bookshop and music venue attracts a bohemian crowd with concerts, seminars and readings. It's open 24 hours, so come for lunch and you'll see bar philosophers wrapping up their vodka-fuelled all-night debates. *40 Nekrasova Ulitsa, T 719 6123, www.platformaclub.ru*

Fasol Café

Tucked away in a basement just south of St Isaac's Square, this café and bar mixes style with comfort, projecting a welcoming glow onto the street outside. Descending into the foyer, the first thing you notice is an illuminated bar top – a typically OTT piece of visual showmanship. Fine service, food and atmosphere make up for stylistic pretensions, which is why, like Krokodil (see p036), Fasol has managed to survive the past few years of relative turmoil in the restaurant scene. Designed by the architect Sergey Shvedov, the interior is complemented by innovative dishes all given a bit of a boost, including sushi, stir fries and traditional Russian fare.
17 Gorokhovaya Ulitsa, T 571 7454, www.fasolcafe.ru

Lobby Bar, Hotel Astoria

The Astoria (see p018) was barely five years old when the revolution threatened to bring down the establishment. Back in 1917, the American communist John Reed was a guest at the hotel as the battles raged outside. Fyodor Lidval's edifice was rapidly renamed the 'Petrograd Military Hotel' and was barricaded – with Reed inside – by angry counter-revolutionaries. These days, the grand setting of St Isaac's Square sees nothing more aggressive than erratically driven minicabs. The Lobby Bar is the best place to sample a traditional Russian afternoon tea in the city, an easy-going venue that will serve you a large pot accompanied by caviar and blinis, plus a dip in the chocolate fountain. Step into the Rotonda Lounge for something stronger. *39 Bolshaya Morskaya Ulitsa, T 494 5757, www.astoria.spb.ru*

Idiot Restaurant

Set in a house on the Moyka, the Idiot is one of Russia's few bona fide vegetarian restaurants. The interior is haphazard and reflects its domestic origins, with tatty chairs, books and defunct electrical equipment all jumbled up together. Luckily, the food and atmosphere more than make up for the seating lucky dip.

82 Naberezhnaya Reki Moyki,
T 315 1675, www.idiot.restoran.ru

Fish Fabrique

One of the city's better cafés and live music clubs, Fish Fabrique is small and intimate, decorated with boldly coloured murals. If that all sounds a bit late 80s Berlin, you'd be right, for the club was an early foray into the alternative arts scene centred around the Pushkinskaya-10 Arts Centre (www. p10.nonmuseum.ru), an artistic squat that was a mainstay of the underground scene from 1989 onwards. Fish moved into the premises in 1998 (when artists Maxim Issaev and Pavel Semtchenko, who work under the AXE name, were let loose on the walls) and soaked up the atmosphere of the six-storey Pushkinskaya, a labyrinth of studios, galleries and installations. The gigs here are cutting edge and the club is the best barometer for what's new.
53 Ligovskiy Prospekt, T 764 4857, www.p10.nonmuseum.ru/fishka

Datscha Bar

Swiftly becoming a favourite among the more laid-back crowd, Datscha is the king of St Petersburg's bar scene, with a wide mix of music from guest DJs. It's a homely place, with the owner herself originally pitching in and DJing. Thursday is new wave night, when things are slightly less hectic and a little more classically old school. Within walking distance of the Grand Hotel Europe (see p017), the bar keeps a low profile even though it stays open until a metro-friendly 6am. Beers from the city's internationally respected brewers help soothe the mind, and once the trains are up and running again, it's time to go home. This kind of venue – small, intimate and unpretentious – has become increasingly popular in the city, and Datscha kick-started the trend.
9 Dumskaya Ulitsa

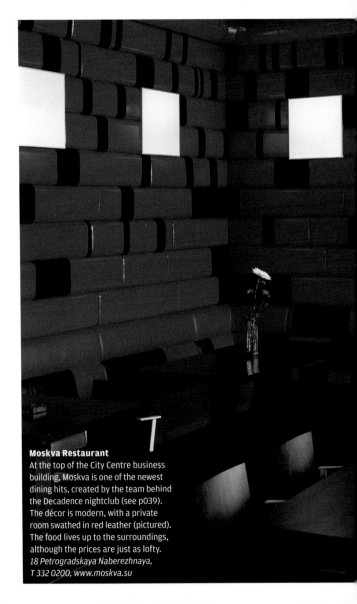

Moskva Restaurant
At the top of the City Centre business
building, Moskva is one of the newest
dining hits, created by the team behind
the Decadence nightclub (see p039).
The décor is modern, with a private
room swathed in red leather (pictured).
The food lives up to the surroundings,
although the prices are just as lofty.
18 Petrogradskaya Naberezhnaya,
T 332 0200, www.moskva.su

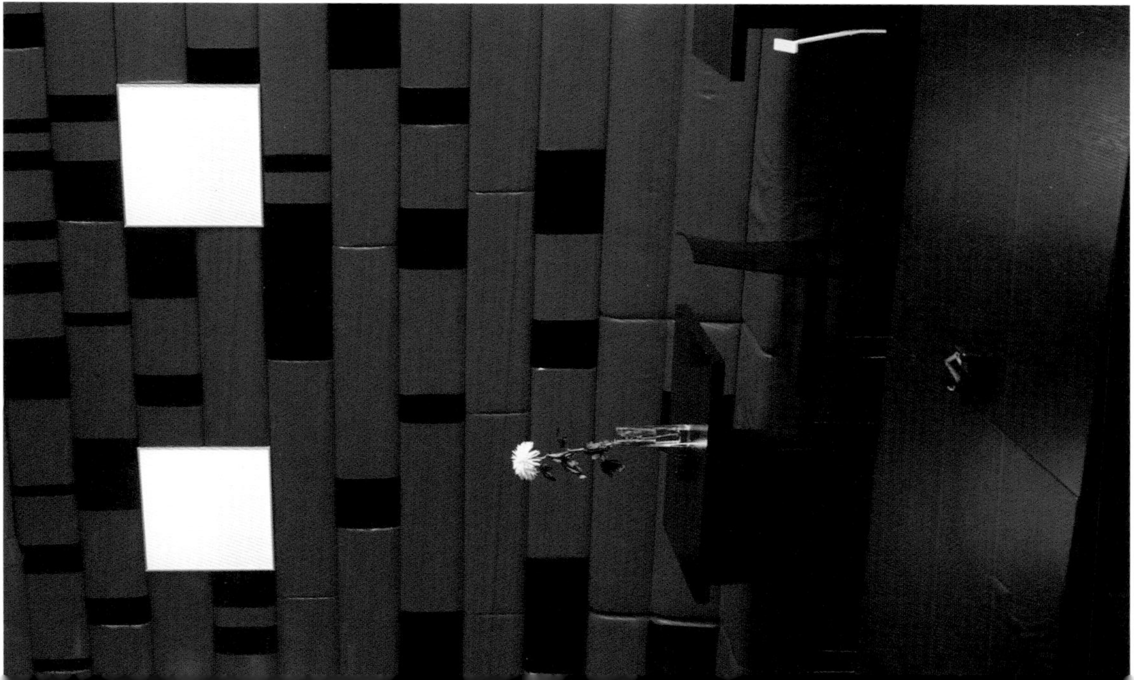

Novus Bar

Opened in 2005 by a former stalwart of
the New York bar scene, Novus is a classic
example of the current vogue for DJ bars.
Located on the second floor above a
shaverma (typical kebab shop), it takes
its name from the novus tables (a Latvian
cross between backgammon and pool)
that have replaced the table football
games found in bars across the city. It's
just 10 minutes walk from the hip nexus
of Fidel Bar (see p058) and Datscha Bar
(see p049), and many of the DJs on the
circuit trudge back and forth entertaining
the young crowd. This consists mostly of
arty students who are looking to kick back
at weekends, yet are still willing to devote
a bit of concentration to a fiercely tricky
game of novus. A good place to spot the
beautiful people who haven't succumbed
to the more pretentious nightspots.
8 Bolshaya Morskaya Ulitsa,
www.novusclub.ru

Dom Aktera

The 'Actor's House' lurks deep within a shabby palace at the upper end of Nevskiy Prospekt. Walk up the grand staircase under the watchful eye of a bust of the great teacher Constantin Stanislavsky and you will step back in time into high Russian culture; this is where students, actors and their tutors come to mull over the day. The food is cheap and cheerful, with cold meats and hot soups served up with great tankards of beer in a dining room that has a school cafeteria-style, no-frills attitude towards furnishings and fittings. It couldn't be more different than the venue downstairs, where the Moorish-themed Magrib café (T 275 7620) switches from serving up daytime doses of foaming cappuccinos into a nightclub with a rather exacting dress code.
84-86 Nevskiy Prospekt, T 272 8395

Onegin

While former stalwarts like Jet Set Club represented St Petersburg bling at its most blinding, more recent clubs have upped the interior ante as a means of attracting the right person. Onegin is another venture by local architect Anton Gorlanov, who goes one louder in the quest to create the most ostentatious interiors (above and overleaf). Mixing baroque decoration with a profusion of mirrors, this restaurant and club is a place to see and be seen. Gorlanov's most recent redesign involved a collaboration with Parisian graffiti artists, and now the baroque splendour has been overloaded with spray paint and street graphics – a quasi-ironic way of trying to shed its élitist image. It hasn't quite worked; this is not the place to buy a cheap bottle of champagne.
11 Sadovaya Ulitsa, T 571 8384

Onegin

Fidel Bar

Next to Datscha (see p049) and owned by Anton Belyankin, a musician with the city's famous ska punk band Dva Samaliota, Fidel is named, of course, after the Cuban dictator. Unlike its neighbour, Fidel is a good size and eschews the dumpster-diving interior aesthetic that is so popular with the arty crowd. Instead, murals by Konstantin Fyodorov cover the walls, the small stage plays host to local indie bands and DJs spin alternative rock classics. It's a familiar formula, but one which is pulled off with enthusiasm. The Soviet Union painted Castro's Cuba as a shining example of how to stand up to the USA, and the owners are slightly guilty of communist nostalgia (club events include a party to celebrate Castro's birthday).
9 Dumskaya Ulitsa

Griboyedov

Founded mid-1990s and overhauled in 2002, Griboyedov is one of the country's best-known clubs, initially taking its cues from the mega-complex so popular in Eastern Europe. It certainly looks the part, housed in an old bomb shelter and therefore quite literally underground (above and overleaf). Like the Fidel Bar (opposite), it's also run by members of local band Dva Samaliota, and Griboyedov exerts a tight grip on the local scene, although visiting clubbers have to adjust to the low ceilings and general feeling of claustrophobia. Wednesdays are disco nights; the dress code is communist kitsch. *2a Voronezhskaya Ulitsa, www.griboedovclub.ru*

INSIDER'S GUIDE

MARINA GISICH, GALLERY OWNER

Siberian-born Marina Gisich arrived in St Petersburg in 1987 to take up a post as a sports teacher, having spent her youth training for Russia's international team of gymnasts. Now heading up the Marina Gisich Gallery (121 Naberezhnaya Reki Fontanki, T 314 4380, www.gisich.com), she also works as an interior designer. Gisich loves the city's up-and-coming fashion boutiques, including Day&Night (6 Malaya Posadskaya Ulitsa, T 234 2300), but for a special occasion, she'll check out the exquisite dresses at Vanity Opera Store (3 Kazanskaya Ulitsa, T 438 5547), before relaxing over a cocktail and panoramic vista from its summer terrace bar.

Her top coffee spot is Aquarel (see p041) for its 'marvellous river views'. A favourite for lunch is Yakitoria (5 Ostrovskogo Ploshchad, T 315 8343), while her best supper venues are Moskva Restaurant (see p050) and the nearby Karavan (46 Voznesenskiy Prospekt, T 310 5678). Gisich takes her foreign guests to sample Russian cuisine at Russkiy Ampir in Stroganov Palace (17 Nevskiy Prospekt, T 571 2409), but she also recommends Sadko (2 Glinki Ploshchad, T 920 8282), which combines modern with traditional. 'After an evening at the Mariinsky (see p038), carry on the fairytale here,' she says. For drinks and dancing, the place to go is Onegin (see p055). Gisich adds: 'Keep an eye out for the occasional parties from Club Arena (2 Konushennaya Ploshchad, T 955 5559).'
For full addresses, see Resources.

ARCHITOUR

A GUIDE TO THE CITY'S ICONIC BUILDINGS

Once the baroque and classical perfection of the original city had given way to Russia's esoteric version of art nouveau – 'style moderne' – it was left to the revolution to usher in the next architectural phase. Constructivism became the de facto style, an abstract, bold take on modernism that was ideal for factories and housing. Sadly, the bulk of this avant-garde movement is now neglected and crumbling, and not helped by Stalin's subsequent espousal of a more monumental, stripped classical idiom. Worse still, the post-war era saw the dog days of Soviet architecture, as apartment blocks swelled in size and impersonality. If you'd like to take in the various districts, pick a sunny day: nothing knocks concrete's dramatic potential on the head like a few drops of rain.

The suburbs are, if anything, worse, being thrown up in an eviscerated post-modernism that has little charm. Stick with the old city and you can feast on muted colours, elegant sculptures and elaborate ironwork. Even the metro is divided between baroque fripperies and 1970s modernism. As a result, your architour will be necessarily varied; for now, the most avant-garde treatments are reserved for interiors, with designers like Anton Gorlanov fusing decorative elements with hard-edged materials to create a new romantic modernism. There's also the prospect of Lord Foster, Rem Koolhaas and Dominique Perrault working in the city.
For full addresses, see Resources.

Sea Passenger Terminal
Designed by architect VA Sokhin, this brutalist structure contains a hotel and ferry terminal for those heading across the Gulf of Finland. Built between 1977 and 1982, it's a notable presence on the quays of Vasilyevskiy Island. The terminal is a chunky piece of late Soviet concrete architecture, with some overt symbolism creeping into the ostensibly functional design – the 'billowing' concrete façade (above) and flowing interior staircase (overleaf) are meant to convey the city's ties to the ocean. The structure has a 78m spire and plenty of dock-side attitude; you can buy a passage to Germany here. For other examples of Soviet brutalism, see the St Petersburg River Yacht Club (T 235 6636) or Hotel Russ (T 273 4683), built around a giant triangular frame.
1 Morskoy Slavy Ploshchad, T 322 1616

Interior, Sea Passenger Terminal

Bolshoi Obukhovsky Bridge

This suspension bridge is arguably the city's most striking contemporary structure, spanning the River Neva close to Obukhovo and Rybatskoe. Constructed in two phases, the first finished in 2006 and the second in 2007, the bridge forms a crucial section of St Petersburg's new ring road. From up high, you can look down over the hydrofoil boatyard, where Soviet-era engineering never looked so purposeful. The Neva and its tributaries are perhaps the most criss-crossed waterways in the world, with some 342 bridges located inside the city limits. These range from the Alexander Nevskiy Bridge, nearly a kilometre long, to the many small footbridges in the city centre.
Oktyabrskaya Naberezhnaya

Church of St John at Chesme Palace

In 1770, this area was a swamp, where, allegedly, Catherine the Great first heard the news of Russia's victory over the Turks in Chesme Bay. Today, on the very same spot, adjacent to the Chesme Palace that the Empress ordered to commemorate the event, St John's (best known as Chesme) Church stands out, an eye-catching, rare example of the gothic revival influence in Russia. Designed by architect Yury Velten in 1780, this stripey, high-windowed structure, decorated with narrow vertical rods, lancet arches and pinnacle turrets, has gone through several restoration phases, even hosting a branch of the Naval Museum before returning to its original use and former glory.
Kamenniy Ostrov

Nevskiy Palace of Culture

You can tell this slab-sided monument to the deepest era of Soviet modernism (it was completed in 1972) is all about glorifying the lives of the workers; the original owner was the Lenin Nevskiy Metal Factory. Designed by EA Levinson and YI Zemtsov, inside there are exhibition spaces and two auditoria, but it's now partly abandoned, used just for clubs and rehearsals. All that official modernism empowered the people, but not how the authorities intended; the building hosted the 1970s exhibition of Unofficial Artists, one of the first strikes against the state trade union. See also the more conventional Gorky Palace of Culture (T 252 7513). *32 Obukhovskoy Oborony Prospekt, T 567 6680*

SHOPPING

THE BEST RETAIL THERAPY AND WHAT TO BUY

Shopping in St Petersburg isn't the most obvious pastime, but visitors are now much better catered for. The multitude of cultural institutions means the choice of souvenirs, books and art historical objects is almost limitless, while the less discerning can pick up *matryoshki* (see p076) in myriad styles. Other specialities include, naturally, vodka, with Flagman (see p083) the local favourite, caviar (see p085) and retro packages of cigarettes (see p084).

If it's fashion you're after, two of the top designers in the city are Tatiana Parfionova (see p074) and Lilia Kisselenko (see p082). Catwalk creations by up-and-coming talent from St Petersburg's art colleges can be snapped up at Defile Boutique (see p078), while the high-tech Gallery of Russian Fashion (Baltiyskiy Fashion Centre, 68 Bolshoy Prospekt, T 322 6713) showcases a multitude of Russian ateliers, among them Princess & Frogs' Elena Tikhonova, Yanis Chamalidi, Larissa Pogoretskaya and Leonid Alexeyev, in 1,500 sq m of brand-new boutique space.

Department stores are headed up by the old-school, Soviet-era DLT, otherwise known as the Leningrad House of Trade (21/23 Bolshaya Konyushennaya Ulitsa, T 318 9502), where they still insist on the archaic ticketed system of buying – collect a stub from one till, then head elsewhere to pay for your item – which seems to be a means of frustrating capitalism at every turn.

For full addresses, see Resources.

Vintage cameras

If you're prepared to hunt, you can find examples of one of St Petersburg's iconic brands in antique shops, junk stores and camera retailers. The Leningrad Optical Mechanical Union, LOMO (Leningradskoye Optiko Mechanichesckoye Obyedinenie) manufactured cameras from the 1930s onwards, almost as a sideline to its core business of lenses, sights and telescopes, many of which were supplied to the Soviet military. Its most celebrated consumer product is the LC-A, a snapshot camera developed in the 1980s. Marketed by an Austrian company, it quickly assumed cult status, but it's the earlier products that are more sought after. You'll also find a host of Russian Leica copies, a market that's still booming and attracting serious collectors from all over the world.
www.lomo.com

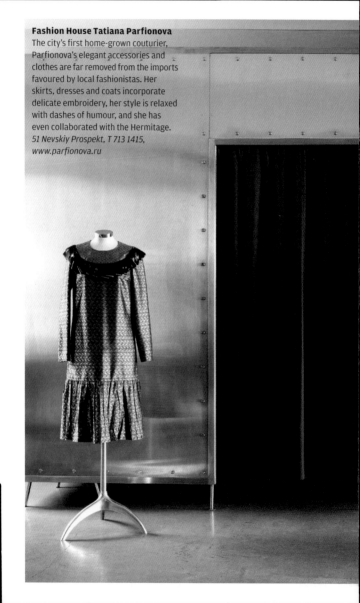

Fashion House Tatiana Parfionova
The city's first home-grown couturier,
Parfionova's elegant accessories and
clothes are far removed from the imports
favoured by local fashionistas. Her
skirts, dresses and coats incorporate
delicate embroidery, her style is relaxed
with dashes of humour, and she has
even collaborated with the Hermitage.
51 Nevskiy Prospekt, T 713 1415,
www.parfionova.ru

Matryoshki

Nesting dolls actually only date back to the 1890s, and were based on a model that came from Japan, but they've swiftly come to be the most recognisable symbol of Russian crafts. The earliest designs were of a group of eight children, ranging from an older girl with a cockerel to a baby in the centre, made from birch and lime, and painted with toxic aniline in yellows and reds. These days, the most common amount of dolls in a set is five, though they can number between seven and 15. The largest *matryoshka* recorded was a 48-piece set painstakingly created in 1913. Sold at souvenir stalls and flea markets all over the city, you can now pick up *matryoshki* in myriad styles and shapes, such as spheres or cones, and sets of dolls diversify into wildly kitsch variants, including miniature Vladimir Putins, Osama Bin Ladens, Harry Potters and even Shreks.

Defile Boutique

This Gostinyy Dvor boutique is more
of a biannual fashion show than a store,
as it sells the collections shown during
Russia's fashion weeks. Everything seen
in the shows, which in St Petersburg take
place in glamorous and architecturally
interesting locations such as the Stroganov
Palace (T 117 2360) and the Museum of
Artillery (T 238 0704), next to the Peter
and Paul Fortress, ends up here. Shop
at Defile to tap into the local fashion
scene and ensure that you come home
with something no one else is likely to
have. The big names in the city, such as
Lilia Kisselenko (see p082) and Princess
& Frogs (T 901 323 3230), all support it.
27 Naberezhnaya Kanala Griboedova,
T 571 9010, www.defilenaneve.ru

Yunona Fair flea market

Russian souvenirs are still dominated by a market for relics of the Soviet era, be they postage stamps, military equipment, hats, badges or even space suits. Although Soviet design and type command respect in the West, most locals don't share that view, and the smart collecting money goes on items associated with contemporary events, such as the 1980 Moscow Olympics. The Games' mascot, Misha, is the world's best-known cuddly communist, mixing a shot-putters' build with Disney emotions. Seek out branded products, from porcelain statuettes to clothing, at flea markets such as Yunona Fair (closed Mondays).

40 Marshala Kazakova Prospekt,
T 784 3441, www.spb-unona.ru

Bolshoy Gostinyy Dvor Shopping Centre

With the dubious honour of being one of the first shopping malls in the world, Bolshoy Gostinyy Dvor is now fragmenting into myriad smaller boutiques. This great bazaar was built between 1757 and 1785, and designed by Francesco Bartolomeo Rastrelli, the Italian-born architect who was commissioned by Empress Elizabeth to create the Winter Palace. Walk around this building beneath its broad arcades and you will clock up nearly one kilometre. Today you can buy almost anything in the complex, with imported goods widely available. It's more fun, however, to soak up the atmosphere and spot the unusual. *35 Nevskiy Prospekt, T 710 5408, www.bgd.ru*

Boutique Lilia Kisselenko

Since showing her first collection in 1991, Kisselenko has become one of the city's most iconic fashion designers, along with Tatiana Parfionova (see p074). Her clothes are still very much haute couture: most of her clients eschew ready-to-wear for a far more tailored, personal service. With a look that's plain and light but also severe and spartan, with sober colours and cuts and the odd ethnic symbol, Kisselenko is adamant that she doesn't cater to mass tastes. Her work is more about the unique quirks of St Petersburg than the demands of the global market, a sense of style that is progressive, with just a hint of austerity.
47 Kirochnaya Ulitsa, T 271 2552, www.kisselenko.ru

Vodka

The spirit is a national speciality, as one might expect, with local brand Flagman (above, 150RUB) favoured by everyday Russians as an accompaniment to almost every meal (it was also the first vodka to get the official Kremlin seal of approval). Flagman is a recent arrival in a crowded market, deliberately designed to appeal to the more traditionalist eye, but the supermarket shelves groan with choice and flavour. *Pertsovka* (pepper vodka) has a particular kick — and we'd recommend stocking up on bottles that appeal to the eye as much as to the taste buds, as there's no shortage of label delights on show.

Cigarette packaging

Russia is very much a booming market for tobacco companies, with domestic players standing their ground against the big four international players and turning every local newspaper kiosk into a miniature museum of packaging options. Marvel at the antediluvian print quality, the striking, timeless graphics and the sheer range that is on offer. For the non-smoker, Russian cigarettes are a great introduction to the ultra-low-budget design collectable, with venerable brands like the space-themed Kosmos and the super-strong Prima jostling for shelf space with heavy-duty versions of Western imports. Our personal favourites are Belomorkanal – just don't, whatever you do, try to smoke them.

Caviar

A recent profusion of upscale stores and delis, such as Yeliseyev Delicatessen (see p086), has provided numerous outlets for this now rare delicacy. Tempting though it might be to snare some from the many street vendors selling cans at knock-down prices, caviar buying here is best done with care – wild sturgeon levels have plummeted, leading to a ban on global imports. Unfortunately, you can pretty much forget about bringing any home. But there's nothing to stop you enjoying a tin or two (300RUB for a 1oz can of sevruga caviar) in the privacy of your hotel room.

Yeliseyev Delicatessen
St Petersburg's demand for high-palate products has been met here since 1898. The shop was the first place many locals saw exotic fruit and vegetables, displayed in an elaborate style moderne building by Gavriil Baranovsky. Presentation is everything, and it's *the* place to stock up on beautifully designed packages and tins. It's also a caviar lover's delight.
56 Nevskiy Prospekt, T 312 1865

SPORTS AND SPAS
WORK OUT, CHILL OUT OR JUST WATCH

Almost all of the city's fitness centres are housed in the basements of the major hotels – Angleterre Hotel (see p026) and Hotel Astoria (see p018) have two of the best, with the Angleterre open to non-guests. Dedicated gyms can be found via the Planet Fitness chain (www.fitness.ru/en). If you're looking for a throwback to the age of bracing dips, the Dunes Sanatorium (see p093) is a Soviet-era structure that promises a total rest cure. For most Russians, R&R is undertaken at the *banyas* (bathhouses) dotted around the city (choose your district carefully, because they can sometimes be unsavoury). An excellent sauna is to be found at the Marshal Hotel (41 Shpalernaya Ulitsa, T 279 9955), available to non-guests for a small fee. That said, the most entrenched sporting traditions tend to be of the hunting, shooting and fishing variety – if it moves or swims, St Petersburg's citizens will blast it or hook it.

For non-participatory thrills, the Russian ice hockey league takes a fair bit of beating; SKA St Petersburg originated as the army team and their reputation precedes them. Sticking with the military theme, if you're feeling especially energetic, shadow the fresh-faced naval cadets as they take time off from sweeping the streets around the Admiralty to continue their infamously arduous training. Just be careful not to fall too closely into step, unless you want to end up scrubbing the Palace Square flagstones.
For full addresses, see Resources.

Petrovskiy Stadium

St Petersburg's answer to Wembley is dominated by its striking lighting towers. Originally built in 1924, it's worth taking a turn around the track to act out your Olympic fantasies. Substantially revised as different styles entered political favour, most recently concrete modernity was switched for a vague classical tilt. Now home to the FC Zenit football team as well as Galaktika Sports Club (T 328 8922), the stadium is one of several major venues on the fringes of the city, including the modern ice-hockey venue New Arena (T 718 6620), the giant Kirov Stadium (T 235 5452) and the Jubileiny Sports Palace (T 719 5615), home to a celebrated figure-skating school.
2g Petrovskiy Ostrov, T 328 8901

Sportivno-Kontsertniy Kompleks
Tennis is big business in the city, with
hundreds of courts added recently, and
the annual ATP St Petersburg Open is
held at this circular sports and leisure
complex, one of the largest covered
stadiums in Europe, seating 25,000.
There are also upscale indoor courts at
the Governor's Tennis Club (T 235 8088)
and the Dinamo Centre (T 235 0170).
8 Yuriya Gagarina Prospekt, T 388 1211

Neptun Sports & Leisure Complex

If you happen to be in the city from November until April when the Neva is frozen over, you can observe the trials and tribulations of local ice fishermen as they drill a hole, sink their line and wait patiently with just a bottle of vodka for company. But swimming doesn't stop with a layer of ice: a local group of year-round masochists known as 'walruses' take the plunge regularly. If you're not keen on joining the ice swimmers, there are plenty of pools, public and private, in the city. Most major hotels can help out, but if not the Hotel Neptun (T 324 4624) offers an extensive sports complex, with Turkish baths and Finnish sauna, while there are also pools at the LDM Health Club and Aquatic Center (T 234 4494).

93a Obvodnogo Kanala Naberezhnaya, T 324 4696, sport.neptun.spb.ru/eng

Dunes, Sestroretsk

St Petersburg's only major golf club is to be found at the Dunes Golf & Country Club (T 437 3874, www.golf.spb.ru), which began life as an 18-hole miniature course (above) in 1995. These days, the nine-hole main course is thronged with new Russians flaunting their latest set of custom clubs. But for real relaxation, we recommend the Dunes Sanatorium Resort, originally constructed in 1979 for party bosses, which explains the ultra-functional Soviet architecture. Located right on the Gulf of Finland, guests enjoy a microclimate, a fine white beach, the eponymous dunes and bright green pine trees. Summertime sees the arrival of the Esco'Bar beach bar, which lures a legion of club-lovers from the city to the sands.
Primorskoye Shosse, T 437 4438, www.dunes.ru

Zimniy Stadion
The 'Winter Stadium', also known by its
original name, Mikhailovsy Manezh, is
a training spot for local athletics teams
and martial arts experts, as well as an
exhibition centre. A military academy
reconstructed by Carlo Rossi in the
1820s, its Soviet-era renovation lingers
on. Check out the Nevskiy Book Forum
for a look inside (www.bookforum.ru).
2 Manezhnaya Ploshchad, T 315 5710

ESCAPES

WHERE TO GO IF YOU WANT TO LEAVE TOWN

The countryside surrounding St Petersburg is rich with cultural and historical treasures, and it provided a rural haven for the early aristrocrats desperate to escape the city in the sweltering summer months. As a result, the Gulf of Finland is the site of some of Russia's most famous palaces, enormous summer retreats built away from city heat and the clouds of fierce mosquitoes that rose up off the former marshland. For more ambitious days out, head up north to Lake Onega (opposite), Lake Ladoga and the White Sea, a landscape of mystical intrigue, steeped in first tsarist and then Bolshevik history. Don't forget that Finland is one hour by plane, and packed with the genius of Alvar Aalto (see po98), while keen sailors have navigated the Volga all the way down to Moscow.

For less exhausting excursions, the palaces are hard to beat, sprawling residences set in mind-blowing gardens, every inch of nature subdued by classic formality. Unfortunately, the upheavals of the 20th century, most notably the city's 880-day siege during WWII, saw the surrounding countryside turned into a wasteland, with even the finest palaces destroyed by the occupying forces. Post-war planning hasn't improved it; huge Brezhnev-era housing projects rise up with grim monotony, and there are intriguing relics of large-scale civil engineering projects that never came off, including a flood barrier that is only now being completed.

For full addresses, see Resources.

Lake Onega

The island-strewn waters of Lake Onega are set in spectacular scenery and have been long favoured by sailing enthusiasts. Petrozavodsk, the capital of the Republic of Karelia, is located on this vast lake, which connects with Lake Ladoga, even larger than Onega and once the site of the 'Road of Life', the transport route across the ice that provided the only access into Leningrad during the WWII siege.

On the small Onegan island of Kizhi sits the spectacular Church of the Transfiguration (above), one of the unsung architectural wonders of the world. Built entirely from wood in the early 18th century, reputedly without the use of a single nail, the structure was the main attraction in an open-air museum of northern Russian wooden architecture set up by the Soviets, and is now a UNESCO World Heritage site.

Alvar Aalto tour, Helsinki

Time spent strolling around modernist masterpieces is time well spent for every design-loving tourist. Helsinki is packed with the brilliancy of local starchitect, the pioneering Alvar Aalto, and is less than an hour's flight from St Petersburg. The crème de la crème of his immense body of work includes two of the city's main attractions, the House of Culture (left and above) and Finlandia Hall

(T 00 358 9 40 241). It's also possible to visit Aalto's former residence (overleaf, T 00 358 9 481 350). If you're feeling a little peckish after all that culture, dine in an Aalto-decorated interior at the Helsinki Savoy Restaurant (T 00 358 9 684 4020). *4 Sturenkatu, T 00 358 9 774 0270, www.kulttuuritalo.fi*

The Aalto House, Helsinki

Peterhof

The summit of Peter the Great's building programme, this great palace continued to be added to throughout the reigns of Elizabeth and Catherine the Great. Best-known for the Grand Cascade of fountains, an aquatic celebration of victory in the Northern War, Peterhof was destroyed in WWII, and left in ruins with thousands of mines scattered around the gardens. Restoration was complete and extensive; the Soviet leaders figuring that although the palace might be a symbol of the hated bourgeoisie, it meant a lot to the Russian spirit. Today, Peterhof is much as it was in its prime. The 176 fountains, as well as the gardens and palaces, are best reached by a half-hour ride on the hydrofoil, a sleek relic of Soviet technology pressed into service from May until late September, from the moorings outside the Hermitage.
2 Razvodnaya Ulitsa, T 427 7425,
www.peterhof.org

NOTES
SKETCHES AND MEMOS

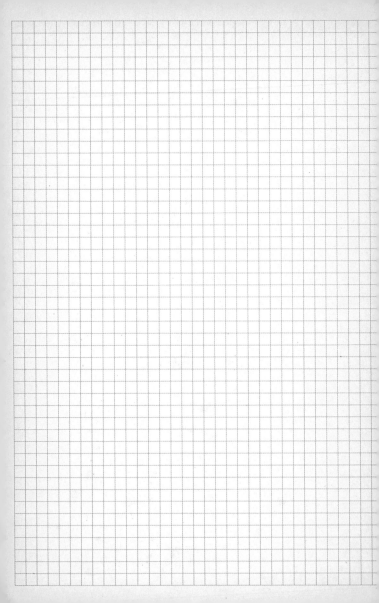

RESOURCES

CITY GUIDE DIRECTORY

HOTELS
ADDRESSES AND ROOM RATES

Alexander House 027
Room rates:
double, from 5,735RUB;
Barcelona Room,
6,600RUB-7,200RUB
27 Naberezhnaya Kryukova Kanala
T 575 3877
www.a-house.ru

Angleterre Hotel 026
Room rates:
double, 10,500RUB;
Deluxe Room, 10,500RUB;
Junior Suite, 22,000RUB;
Senator Suite,
32,000RUB-40,000RUB
24 Bolshaya Morskaya Ulitsa
T 494 5666
www.angleterrehotel.com

Art Hotel 030
Room rates:
double, 2,500RUB-4,000RUB;
Junior Suite, 3,200RUB;
Suite, 4,000RUB
27/29 Mokhovaya Ulitsa
T 740 7585
www.art-hotel.ru

Corinthia Nevskij Palace Hotel 021
Room rates:
double, 10,000RUB-11,250RUB
57 Nevskiy Prospekt
T 380 2001
www.corinthia.ru

Eliseev Palace Hotel 020
Room rates:
double, 14,750RUB-19,000RUB
Eliseev Suite, 58,000RUB-72,000RUB
59 Naberezhnaya Reki Moyki
T 324 9911
www.eliseevpalacehotel.com

Grand Hotel Europe 017
Room rates:
double, from 12,000RUB;
Lidval Suite, from 24,000RUB
1/7 Mikhaylovskaya Ulitsa
T 329 6000
www.grandhoteleurope.com

Hotel Astoria 018
Room rates:
double, 6,000RUB;
Rooms 715-724, 12,000RUB;
Presidential Suite, 82,000RUB
39 Bolshaya Morskaya Ulitsa
T 494 5757
www.astoria.spb.ru

Kempinski Hotel Moika 22 023
Room rates:
double, 6,800RUB-9,600RUB;
River View Executive Suite,
37,400RUB-74,800RUB
22 Naberezhnaya Reki Moyki
T 335 9111
www.kempinski-st-petersburg.com

Rachmaninov Antique Hotel 024
Room rates:
double, 3,700RUB;
Rachmaninov Lux,
8,000RUB-10,700RUB
5 Kazanskaya Ulitsa
T 571 7618
www.kazansky5.com

Renaissance St Petersburg Baltic Hotel 022
Room rates:
double, 5,800RUB-12,300RUB;
bi-level suite, 20,000RUB-25,400RUB
4 Pochtamtskaya Ulitsa
T 380 4000
www.marriott.com

Residence Taleon Sheremetev Palace 020
Room rates:
double, 17,000RUB
4 Naberezhnaya Kutuzova
T 324 9911
www.sheremetevpalace.com

WALLPAPER* CITY GUIDES

Editorial Director
Richard Cook

Art Director
Loran Stosskopf

City Editor
Jonathan Bell

Associate Writer
Dimitry Pervushin

Project Editor
Rachael Moloney

**Executive
Managing Editor**
Jessica Firmin

Chief Designer
Ben Blossom

Designer
Ingvild Sandal

Map Illustrator
Russell Bell

Photography Editor
Christopher Lands

Photography Assistant
Jasmine Labeau

Chief Sub-Editor
Jeremy Case

Sub-Editor
Siân Lyde

Assistant Sub-Editor
Milly Nolan

Interns
Hayley Leaver
Jill Philips

**Wallpaper* Group
Editor-in-Chief**
Jeremy Langmead

Creative Director
Tony Chambers

Publishing Director
Fiona Dent

Contributors
Paul Barnes
Jeroen Bergmans
Alan Fletcher
Sara Henrichs
David McKendrick
Claudia Perin
Meirion Pritchard
James Reid
Ellie Stathaki

PHAIDON

Phaidon Press Limited
Regent's Wharf
All Saints Street
London N1 9PA

Phaidon Press Inc
180 Varick Street
New York, NY 10014
www.phaidon.com

First published 2007
© 2007 Phaidon
Press Limited

ISBN 978 0 7148 4729 0

A CIP Catalogue record
for this book is available
from the British Library.

All prices are correct at
time of going to press,
but are subject to change.

Printed in China

PHOTOGRAPHERS

Antoine Gyori/Corbis
St Petersburg city view,
inside front cover

Frank Herfort
Finland Station, p013
Kempinski Hotel Moika 22,
p023
Rachmaninov Antique
Hotel, p024, p025
Angleterre Hotel, p026
Alexander House, p027,
pp028-029
Art Hotel, p030, p031
Russian Museum, p033
Beluga Silver & Amber
Boutique, p034
St Isaac's Cathedral, p035
Krokodil, pp036-037
Mariinsky Theatre, p038
Decadance, p039
Aquarel, p041
Platforma Art Café,
pp042-043
Fasol Café, p044
Idiot Restaurant,
pp046-047
Fish Fabrique, p048
Novus Bar, pp052-053
Dom Aktera, p054
Onegin, p055
Fidel Bar, p058
Griboyedov, pp060-061
Interior, Sea Passenger
Terminal, pp066-067
Bolshoi Obukhovsky
Bridge, p068

Church of St John at
Chesme Palace, p069
Fashion House Tatiana
Parfionova, pp074-075
Defile Boutique, p078
Bolshoy Gostinyy Dvor
Shopping Centre,
pp080-081
Boutique Lilia Kisselenko,
p082
Yeliseyev Delicatessen,
pp086-087
Petrovskiy Stadium, p089
Sportivno-Kontsertniy
Kompleks, pp090-091
Dunes, Sestroretsk, p093
Zimniy Stadion,
pp094-095

**Maija Holma/Alvar
Aalto Museum**
House of Culture, Helsinki,
p099
The Aalto House, Helsinki,
pp100-101

**Martti Kapanen/Alvar
Aalto Museum**
House of Culture, Helsinki,
p098

Igor Sakharov
Vintage cameras, p073
Matryoshki, pp076-077
Yunona Fair flea market,
p079
Vodka, p083
Cigarette packaging, p084
Caviar, p085

Daniel Stier
The Hermitage, pp010-011
Church on Spilled Blood,
p012
Departure Hall, Finland
Station, pp014-015
Grand Hotel Europe, p017
Renaissance St Petersburg
Baltic Hotel, p022
Datscha Bar, p049
Moskva Restaurant,
pp050-051
Onegin, pp056-057
Marina Gisich, p063
Sea Passenger Terminal,
p065
Nevskiy Palace of Culture,
pp070-071
Peterhof, pp102-103

ST PETERSBURG
A COLOUR-CODED GUIDE TO THE HOT 'HOODS

VASILYEVSKIY ISLAND
Peter the Great's vision of Venice boasts canals and bridges and the city's oldest buildings

PETROGRADSKAYA STORONA
Aleksandrovskiy Park and the Peter and Paul Fortress are the foil to hip clubs and shops

SENNAYA PLOSHCHAD
Upmarket boutiques line Viznesenskiy Prospekt with bijou property along Fontanka canal

PALACE EMBANKMENT
The Hermitage, the Church on Spilled Blood and the Winter Palace are absolute must-sees

GOSTINYY DVOR
The main shopping street, Nevskiy Prospekt, dominates with its awe-inspiring architecture

NEW HOLLAND
These 18th-century navy-owned warehouses are being redeveloped into a cultural centre

ADMIRALTY
The imposing Admiralty building stands proudly at the epicentre of the modern city

For a full description of each neighbourhood,
including the places you really must not miss, see the Introduction